Beloved, Let's Get the Rapture Right!

Aaron B. Claxton, PhD

Beloved, Let's Get the Rapture Right!

Copyright © 2016 by Aaron B. Claxton

All rights reserved. No part of this book may be reproduced, stored in retrieval system, or transmitted in any form or by any means – electronic, mechanical, photocopy, recording, or otherwise – except for brief quotations in printed reviews, without written permission of the author.

Unless otherwise noted, Scripture is taken from The Holy Bible, The King James Version (KJV). The King James Version is in the public domain.

ISBN: 978-0-9964040-9-9

Published by Kingdom Kaught Publishing, LLC
Odenton, MD 21113

First Printing 2015
Printed in the USA

DEDICATION

It gives me great pleasure to dedicate this book to my beloved and indispensable wife, of nearly 58 years. She is not only my lover, and confidante, but also my helper, critic and encourager in everything I do- including this book.

She is forever my proofreader, advisor and all that I have ever needed in this business of book writing.

Dr. Deborah J. Claxton has earned several degrees and has of late received her doctorate of Religious Education-and is an author in her own right.

Thank God for "Dr. Deborah," as she is affectionately known by many, and "Sugar Lump," as she is known by me.

Beloved, Let's Get the Rapture Right!

Several weeks ago the Lord visited me with His glorious presence, while I was praying. He impressed me with the thought of writing my thirty-third (33rd) book on the subject of *Getting the Rapture Right!*

Nearly 60 years ago the Lord opened my eyes to the *simple truth* about the Rapture of the church. I am 82 years of age, and since a child I heard teachings on the Rapture that caused me some concern. My Sunday school teachers and other Bible teachers "drilled" it into my head that Jesus' feet would not touch the earth in the Rapture. Instead, they said that He would come to the mid-air and prepared believers would be caught up to meet Him there. They taught us that at that point Christ would take the raptured saints to heaven for seven years; others said Christ would take the raptured saints to heaven for a 1,000 year "honeymoon." To say the least, such teachings were confusing, and today the *Pre-tribulationists* are still teaching that

Christ will *return* (in the Rapture) *before* the great tribulation.

Here's where I parted company with such teachings fifty plus (50+) years ago. I discovered Christ's own teachings that say that His second (2nd) coming or return will take place *immediately after the tribulation* of those days (not before) (Matthew 24:29-31). This *Post-tribulational* view of Christ's return and the Rapture of the church is consistently taught in the New Testament Scriptures! The *Pre-tribulational* view of the Rapture of the Church is erroneous, foreign and is the result of men *eisegeting* their ideas into the Scriptures on this subject rather than simply allowing the Bible to speak for itself. These men (Dr. Scofield, Dr. Darby et al.) attempted to expound on the Rapture *before the time!* Daniel was told to wait until *the end of days* for proper understanding.

The aforementioned men, i.e. Dr. C.I. Scofield, Dr. John Darby, et.al, who lived and wrote in the 1800's, attempted to expound on the Rapture *before the time!* Daniel was told by God, "but you, Daniel, shut up the words, and seal up the book until *the time of the end…*, and *knowledge shall increase.*" And verse nine of that chapter goes on to say: "Go your way, Daniel, for the words (of your prophecies) are *closed up* and *sealed till the time of the end"* (Dan. 12:9).

There we have it. The writings of Daniel, the prophecies given to him, would *be* closed up and sealed *until the time of the end.* Well, can we know or have an idea of when the time of the end will be? I would say yes! Jesus in his Olivet Discourse, cited the Israelites and their *repossessing Jerusalem* as *an endtime sign worth noting.* In Luke 21:23-24, Jesus said: "For there will be great distress in the land and wrath upon this people. And they will fall by the edge of the sword, and be led away captive unto all nations (in 70 A.D.) And Jerusalem will be trampled by the Gentiles *until the times of the Gentiles are fulfilled."*

Jesus was reaching back to the book of Daniel with his comments about Jerusalem being trampled under the feet of the Gentiles, *until the times of the Gentiles be fulfilled.* King Nebuchadnezzar had two dreams. One was about a huge statue consisting of four kingdoms (or empires) which would be Gentile. And they would rule the world for thousands of years. But Daniel wrote: "And in the days of these kings (kingdoms) the God of heaven (Yaweh) will set up a kingdom which shall never be destroyed; and the kingdom shall be left to other people; (Old and New Testament saints) it shall break in pieces and consume all these (Gentile) kingdoms; and it shall stand forever". (Daniel 2:44). The other dream of the king was about four beasts, representing the same four Gentile kingdoms which will also be destroyed by the Living God.

Those four Gentile kingdoms were Babylon, Medo-Persia, Greco-Roman and Islam. All had trampled on Jerusalem until the 1967 war between Egypt and Israel. This is when Egypt attacked Israel, after which, Israel regained control of Jerusalem for the *first time* since 70 A.D., during the time of The Roman invasion of Jerusalem.

Beloveds, it seems clear to me that *1967 is the time* both Jesus and Daniel (words to him) were referring to as *the time of the end.* Gentile rule of Jerusalem ended at that time. To me that would be the *beginning of the time of the end.* Prior to that time men would simply be guessing about the timing of *end-time* events. It was around that time (the early 1960's) that the Lord began to open my eyes about end-time events-the Rapture and the Second Coming, etc. I am not the only one for whom God began to cause "Knowledge to be increased" about the end times. Scholars of end-time truth like Walid Shoebat ("God's War on Terror, the Bible, Prophecy and Islam"); and Joel Richardson,

("The Islamic Antichrist") et al, were also given this revelation.. Other notable scholars/authors who got the Rapture right would be: Dr. George E. Ladd, and Dr. William E. Anderson.

Great men of God like Dr. C.I. Scoefield and Dr. John Darby could have avoided their *Pretribulation errors*, if they had only read and believed what the Risen Lord gave to the Apostle Paul, which he recorded in I Thessalonians, and especially II Thessalonians, concerning the *timing* of the Rapture and the Second Coming of our Lord Jesus Christ. If those scholars had simply referred to Paul's words in II Thessalonians 2:1-3, which say: "Now, brethren, concerning *the coming* of our Lord Jesus Christ and *our gathering together to Him* (the Rapture)"...Let no one deceive you by any means; for *that day* (same day) will not come unless the falling away comes first, and *the man of sin is revealed*, the son of perdition." Please understand that the man of sin, the Antichrist, will bring great persecution (tribulation) upon the church; and he will be destroyed by Jesus Christ our Lord at His Second Coming, when He catches the church up to meet Him in air. Verse 8 of II Thessalonians chapter 2 says, "And then the lawless one will be revealed, whom the Lord will consume with the breath of His mouth and destroy with the brightness of His Coming".

I am certain that the Lord has commissioned me to write a *simple treatise* on this subject, which well-meaning men of God have complicated and made difficult. The Lord wants me to *simplify* the subject of the Rapture of the church. To begin with, let us first of all state that the word *Rapture* does not appear in the Bible per se. The apostle whom Christ chose to expound on this subject is *the Apostle Paul.* Paul coined the expression "caught up to meet" in 1 Thessalonians 4:17, when he wrote: "Then we who are alive and remain shall be *caught up together* with them (the dead in Christ) in the cloud to *meet the Lord* in the air." The Greek word for "caught up" which Paul used here is *harpazo,* which means "to seize, to catch up or away, to pluck, to take by force". (Strong's Concordance of the Bible, page 16, Greek New Testament, #726).

"Raptures" or *translations* took place in Bible, in Old Testament times, such as in the cases of both Enoch and Elijah. Enoch's *translation to heaven* by God is written in Genesis 5:24. The word says, "And Enoch walked with God; and *he was not, for God took him* to heaven" *(Emphasis mine).* Elijah's translation from earth to heaven is recorded in 2 Kings 2:11 as follows: "Then it happened, as they continued on and talked (Elijah and Elisha) that suddenly a chariot of fire appeared with horses of fire, and separated the two of them; and Elijah *went up* in a whirlwind *into heaven.*" Again, well-meaning preachers and Bible teachers teach that Christ is going to take the Church up to heaven in the Rapture. This is *erroneous* and *untrue!* They have imagined from the Old Testament accounts that this is what happens when Christ snatches the church up to meet Him *in the air!* Some *Pre-trib* Christian camps have gone so far as to say, "We're going up in the first load". How sad! This too is *unbiblical!*

Let us now examine the *simple truth* that the Apostle Paul wrote on the subject of the Rapture of the Church. Paul is noted for his long, run on sentences in his epistles. An example of Paul's long run on sentences can be found in the sentence (or thought) that begins in Romans 8:17 and ends in Romans 8:37. In like manner, Paul begins his thought about Christ's Second Coming in I Thessalonians 3:13 when he writes: "So that He may establish your hearts blameless in holiness before our God and Father at *the coming of our Lord* Jesus Christ *with all His saints."* Here Paul speaks of the return of the Lord as *the coming of the Lord.* The expression "with all His saints" is comprehended in I Thessalonians 4:14 which says, "For if we believe that Jesus died and rose again, even so God *will bring with Him those who sleep in Jesus.*" Those who sleep in Jesus are a part of "all His saints" as recorded in I Thessalonians 3:13. The holy angels are also a part of "all his saints" who return with Christ in His Second Coming. Paul wrote the following in his Second Epistle to the Thessalonians: "Since it is a righteous thing with God to repay with tribulation (retribution) those who trouble you, and give you who are troubled (in tribulation) *rest with us, when the Lord Jesus is revealed from heaven with His mighty angels* in flaming fire…" (II Thessalonians 2:6-8). We see here that Christ's mighty angels are with Him when He is revealed, as a part of "all His saints" (or holy ones) in I Thessalonians 3:13. Note also that the Rapture and Second Coming will not be silent as the *Pretriblers* teach. It will be noisy with mighty angels in flaming fire.

Now the *timing* of Christ's return *is the same time* as the Rapture of the church – *not seven years later* as the Pretribulationists erroneously teach! In that same chapter one of II Thessalonians when Paul speaks of Christ being revealed in verse 7, he also says: "When He comes *in that Day to be glorified* in the saints" *(verse*

10). The revealing and glorifying happens on the same Day!

Allow us, at this point, to cite other co-related Scripture passages to this one in II Thessalonians 1:10 which references *glorification* in the Rapture. Paul speaks in Romans 8:17 and says, "…if indeed we suffer with Him (Christ) that we may be *glorified together*," and in Romans 8:18, of "the glory that will be revealed in us." In 1 Corinthians 15:51-52, the Apostle Paul wrote: "We shall not all sleep, but *we will all be changed* – in a moment, in the twinkling of an eye, <u>at the last trump</u>. For the trumpet shall sound, the dead will be raised imperishable, and we shall be changed." The *being changed* equals glorification! In Philippians 3:20-21, Paul wrote, "For our citizenship is in heaven, <u>from which</u> we also eagerly await for the Savior, the Lord Jesus Christ, who will transform our lowly body that it may *be conformed to His glorious body* according to the working by which He is able even to subdue all things to Himself". Paul wrote the following concerning our glorification at the time of His Coming and the Rapture: *"When Christ* who is our life *appears, then you will appear with Him in glory"* (Colossians 3:4). Finally, we cite that famous verse in 1 John 3:2: "Beloved, now are we the children (the sons) of God; and it has not yet been revealed what we shall be (like) but we know that when he is revealed, (in the Rapture and the Second Coming) *we shall be like Him*, for we shall see Him as He is."

Then in II Thessalonians 2:1 *Paul connects the 2nd Coming of Christ and the Rapture of the Church* as though they are *one event* taking place at the same time! Here's what Paul wrote in II Thessalonians 2:1, "Now, brethren, concerning, the coming of our Lord Jesus Christ and *our gathering together to Him*; (The latter is the Rapture) we ask you not to be shaken in mind or troubled… as though the day of Christ (the Lord) had come" (II Thessalonians 2:1-2). A false message had been circulated among the Thessalonians, purporting to be from Paul, that the Day of Christ or the Lord had already come. Once again from this text, what is *the Day* of Christ? According to Paul, *that Day is the coming of the Lord and our gathering together to Him"* (2 Thessalonians 2:1). It is *the Coming* of the Lord and *the Rapture* of the church, which Paul presents as *one* and *the same event! No separation of seven years between the two parts of the event.*

Paul sets forth *two things* that must happen *before* "that Day" comes. Paul wrote: "Let no one deceive you *by any means;* for *that Day* (the day of Christ's coming and the day of our gathering to Him (the Rapture) will not come unless *the falling away* (the apostasy) comes first and *the man of sin* (the *anti-Christ*) is revealed (second), the son of perdition." (2 Thessalonians 2:3). (Emphases mine).

Once again we say, we *need not* seek any other Bible writer or Old Testament prophets (Daniel, Ezekiel, etc.) to learn about the Rapture of the Church. Jesus, the Risen Lord gave the revelation of the Rapture of the church *exclusively* to His servant the *Apostle Paul.* You will *notice* that no other New Testament apostle tackles the subject of the Rapture directly, as the Apostle Paul does. Oh yes, the Apostle John makes a veiled reference to two unnamed witnesses of the Lord in Revelation 11:12, who were killed, resurrected and *translated* to heaven. John wrote, "And they ascended to heaven in a cloud, and their enemies *saw* them." Yes, but this is *not* the Rapture of the Church!

Again, we read about the *translation of John* from earth to heaven in Revelation 4:1-2. He wrote: "After these things I looked, and behold, a door standing open in heaven. And the voice which I heard was like a trumpet speaking *with me* saying, 'Come up here, and I will show you things which must take place after this.' Immediately I was in the Spirit; and behold, a throne set in heaven, and one sat on the throne". For many years the Pretribulationist brethren have insisted that this event is "in fact" the Rapture of the Church! How wrong they are, and how wrong they have been! John uses the personal pronoun "I." He said, "I looked," "I heard," and "I was in the Spirit." What part of "I" don't they understand? The church is *nowhere* mentioned in these passages! These passages are similar to Ezekiel's experience in the Lord. Ezekiel said: "So the Spirit lifted me up and took me away…the hand of the Lord was strong upon me". (Ezekiel 3:14). Surely these passages in no way suggest that Ezekiel is *the whole house of Israel!* Neither does John's experience in Revelation 4:2-3 in anyway suggest that he is *the raptured church of Jesus Christ!* Oh! The extremes to which men will go to make their concocted doctrines or "cunningly devised fables" work!

John references one other earth to heaven translation in Revelation chapter 12 verse 5. This verse says "She (a woman who was a heavenly sign, who was clothed with the sun, with the moon under her feet, etc.) bore a male Child who was to rule all nations with a rod of iron. And her Child was *caught up* (translated) to God and His throne." This is an obvious reference to *Jesus the Christ* who ascended from earth to heaven, to the throne of God. (1 Peter 3:21-22 and Psalm 2:7-

12, *Emphases mine*). The mystery woman represents Israel.

If there are other "Raptures" in the Bible, I am not aware of them. Again, the Lord has commissioned me to *simplify* the teaching on the Rapture of the church, where men have made this subject deep, mysterious and complicated. Some Christian songs have added to the confusion of the Rapture of the Church. Some of those songs would be: "I'm Going Away." I ask, *away* where? Are you going away from the earth in death? Another song says, "I'm Going up Yonder to Be with My Lord." Is this also a song about death, and going up to heaven? Allow me to cite one more old Christian song, It says, "There's going to be a *meeting in the air*, in the sweet, sweet bye and bye, and I'm going to meet, to meet you over there in that land *beyond the sky...*" Although this song speaks of a meeting in the air, it goes on to say the meeting is *"beyond the sky"* and *"over there."* This song also becomes extra biblical. The Bible simply says, "...and the dead in Christ (Christians whose bodies are in their graves) shall rise first. Then we who are alive and remain shall be *caught up* (raptured) together with them in the clouds (the atmospheric heaven) *to meet* the Lord in the air. And thus we shall always be with the Lord" (1 Thessalonians 4:17).

I believe much of the confusion surrounding the Rapture of the Church comes from old mind sets that people have drawn from the Old Testament and prophets who were *translated* from the earth to heaven. Yes, Jesus was *translated* from earth to heaven according to Dr. Luke's account in Acts 1:9 and 11. He wrote: "Now when He (Jesus) had spoken things, while they watched, He was *taken up,* and a cloud received Him out of their sight…This same Jesus, who was *taken up from you into heaven,* will come in like manner as you saw Him *go into heaven.*"

What then is the *difference* between the Bible *translations* of prophets and Jesus from earth to heaven, and the Rapture of the church? I could just refer you to my second book on eschatology entitled "Caught Up to Meet Him." The whole emphasis of the Rapture of the church is that it is a *meeting* of Christ with His church in the air. Part of Christ's Church is with Him as He departs from heaven. Those saints, the dead in Christ, whom we call the "church triumphant," are in heaven with Christ, and they return to the *midair* with Him. The other part of Christ's bride is on the earth, "the church militant," awaiting Christ's return and arrival, to deliver them from the wrath of Satan in the great tribulation (Rev. 12:12-17). Paul gives us a pictorial witness of this event. He says, "God is just: He will pay back trouble to those who trouble you *and give relief to you who are troubled (persecuted),* and to us as well. This will happen *when the Lord Jesus is revealed from heaven* in blazing fire with his powerful angels...*on the day he comes to be glorified in his holy people"* (2 Thessalonians 1:6, 10, NIV Bible).

Again, what is the difference between Rapture and translation? With *translations* as we have described them from the Bible, men *changed their location* (Enoch, Elijah, John, Jesus and the two witnesses) from *earth to heaven!* In the *Rapture,* the earth dwelling saints ascend to the *midair,* and are *glorified by Christ there!* See 2 Thessalonians 1:2 and, I Thessalonians 4:14-18. Beloveds, this is what the Bible says in plain English! I will not add to it nor take anything from it (Revelation 22:18-19).

Thus we have plainly and clearly given you the *biblical distinctions* between the translation of Old Testament saints from earth to heaven; and the Rapture of the church which is caught up to the Lord *in the air* and *remains forever with Him.* The raptured saints then continue with Christ in His descent to earth to punish the *wicked* and then *to establish His earthly kingdom,* wherein He shall reign one thousand years. And we shall reign with Him. The Apostle John wrote: "Blessed and holy is he who has part in the first resurrection. Over such the second death has no power, but they shall be priests of God and of Christ, and *shall reign with Him a thousand years"* (Rev. 20:6). Revelation 5:10b says, "We shall reign on the earth".

We pray to Christ that we have made the distinction plain between <u>Bible translations from earth to heaven</u>, and <u>the Rapture of the church</u>, wherein *the church militant on earth* is caught up to *meet the Lord*, and *the church triumphant, descending* with Christ from heaven. The two parts of the church are *glorified together,* in the midair in Christ's presence, and continue with Him in His descent to the earth.

This completes the "Beloved, Let's Get the Rapture Right!" Even so, Come Lord Jesus!(Rev.22:20) We pray that your eyes will be anointed to see; your heart opened to receive; your mind ready to grasp, and your spirit will be illuminated with truth after reading this booklet.

Suggested Readings:
1. "Rapture? Sure…but when?" by William E. Anderson
2. "A Commentary on THE REVELATION OF JOHN" by Dr. George E. Ladd
3. "The Biblical View of the Rapture and the Second

Beloved, Let's Get the Rapture Right!

Coming" by Dr. Aaron B. Claxton
4. "Caught Up to Mee t Him" by Dr. Aaron B. Claxton

www.ingramcontent.com/pod-product-compliance
Lightning Source LLC
Chambersburg PA
CBHW052132010526
44113CB00034B/1907